GW00568033

The Frames

behind the glass

Zoran Orlić is a Croatian-born fine arts photographer with a flair for revealing the many moods of rock photography. Orlić's passion for the camera and music has led him to capture rock bands on film for the last seventeen years. Most recently noted for his work with Wilco, Orlić's snapshots have appeared in numerous magazines, newspapers, websites and music packaging.

The Frames
behind the glass

photographed by Zoran Orlić

text by Zoran Orlić with Janine Schaults

The Collins Press

Published in 2006 by
The Collins Press
West Link Park
Doughcloyne
Wilton
Cork

British Library Cataloguing in Publication Data

Orlić, Zoran
The Frames : behind the glass
1. Frames (Musical group) 2. Rock musicians - Ireland -
Biography
I. Title II. Schaults, Janine
782.4'2166'0922

ISBN-10: 1-905172-32-X
ISBN-13: 978-1905172-320

Font: Gill Sans 14 point

Text and cover design: Michael Bom, Bom Design, Rotterdam, www.bomdesign.nl

Front cover image: The Frames in New York City, 2004
Back cover image: The Frames, Lemont, Illinois, 2002

Printed in Malta

Acknowledgements Without a start you get nowhere ... I first and foremost want to thank Glen Hansard for reading, appreciating and responding to my crazed fan mail, which started these unforgettable memories and images.

Thanks to the musicians − Glen Hansard, Colm Mac Con Iomaire, Joe Doyle, Rob Bochnik, Dave Hingerty, David Odlum, Graham Downey, John Carney, Noreen O'Donnell, Paul Brennan-Binzer and Johnny Boyle − for creating music that feeds my soul. This passion has given life to the photography in this book, and has brought me to a level of happiness not many people are lucky enough to experience at such close range.

Thanks to Claire Leadbitter for all her love, hard work and endless co-ordination. Claire has patiently manoeuvred most of my Frames' experiences from the sidelines − thank you for everything.

Thanks also to Gerard McDonnell, the King of Sound and Zen.

My legal Zen Master Roy H. Wyman Jr. for holding my hand through complete darkness.

Janine Schaults' translation made my storytelling easy and comprehensible. Watch out for her name − her ambition is powerful and convincing. This is our first and I have a feeling that it's not our last!

I am very grateful to Zlata Kožul Naumovski, aka 'Charlie' and sometimes − in moments like this − 'Angel,' for her editing skills. Without her dissecting eye the text never would have made sense.

Michael Bom and Antoinet Deurloo of Bom Design are the most creative designer folks I know and deserve special thanks. It was only natural that I begged them to design the book with me via Rotterdam. The opportunity to work with them has been a dream come true!

Huge thanks to Mike Mondschein, aka 'Jim,' for being my music and adventure partner over the years. From the hours of basement Rush sessions, to the nacho-targeted bicycle journeys, to the Kicker-driven Colt audio machine and then finally graduating to an aircraft for exploration, you have always been there, Jim!

A very special thanks to Stipe and Mare Orlić for buying me the first serious SLR back in 1979 that has fired my curiosity ever since. And also a huge thanks to the Orlić family in Chicago and Croatia.

This book is dedicated to Anita, who − thank God − stumbled into FitzGerald's one night and caught a Frames gig by complete accident! A couple of years later we eventually met at a Chicago Frames gig, which led to her becoming my wife, love and saviour.

And finally to my spiritual leader, Luce Rudić (aka Baba Luce).

Zoran Orlić, July 2006

Planting the seed No high has seduced my mind or affected my spirit like the experience of first discovering the music of The Frames and then ultimately surrendering to it. Simply put, The Frames are the only band for which I'd risk embarrassment, travel the globe and babble incessantly about to all who will listen, even strangers. Well, mostly strangers. If it sounds like I'm a fanatic, it's because I am. I'm also a photographer and I've documented the musical journey of one of the most exciting rock bands playing today.

It began in 1983 with U2. Sixteen years old, listening to my father's Grundig shortwave radio, 'New Year's Day' shot out through the speakers in all its immediacy and jagged edges. Gripped with curiosity, I sought out all information on U2 and the country from which they hailed. This insatiable drive didn't end with Bono's mullet; it led me to immerse myself in the sounds of Ireland. Bands such as Cactus World News, The Fat Lady Sings and An Emotional Fish captivated my mind and soul. In the same way baseball and football fanatics quote players' stats, I took pride in my ability to list the discography of Dublin. Vintage Vinyl in Evanston, Illinois, a whopping 45-minute drive from my Chicago home, amazingly stocked these 'rare' bands from Ireland and the UK. This local record shop, fiercely loyal to independent labels, became a touchstone and connected me to a land out of reach.

At long last, in 1990, I finally reached the city at the centre of my musical obsessions during a college exchange programme in the Netherlands. None of my expectations compared to setting foot in Dublin. I felt as comfortable on the island of Ireland as I did on my beloved Dalmatian coast of Croatia where I was born. Holding the most current issue of *Hotpress* (instead of reading a month-old copy in Chicago), drinking pints of Guinness and shot after shot of Paddy's at Dockers, naively expecting to find U2 sitting at the next table – life didn't get any better.

My first and second attempts at writing fan letters to An Emotional Fish and The Fat Lady Sings proved successful as the bands surprisingly wrote back. I soon found out that An Emotional

Fish was headlining at Park West, a mid-size venue on Chicago's North Side. During the show, spiked with enormous energy, lead singer Gerard Whelan pulled several fans, including myself, onto the stage to dance like fools. Later the entire band and I, plus several buddies, defied the limitations of space by squeezing into my friend's Volkswagen Jetta, which deposited us at the famous Chicago blues club, Kingston Mines.

I even managed to take some random road trips with a few Irish acts. With my friend Mike Mondschein in tow, I made a six-hour trek to London, Canada, to see The Fat Lady Sings. The band was impressed and slightly stunned that we travelled such a long distance for five Irish rockers barely known in North America. A few days later, when The Fat Lady Sings arrived in Chicago for a series of gigs, they readily encouraged me to join them for a week to snap some shots of their tour. Looking back, I had unknowingly planted the seed for my wildest dream. Only a couple years later another fan letter would serve to bring this dream to reality.

A magazine review of a band called The Frames caught my eye in Chicago several years after Dublin. I was pleased to see that they were an Irish band and coincidentally produced by Gil Norton of Pixies fame, one of my favourite bands ever. These two factors were enough to hurl me to the record shop. The 1992/93 review of 'Another Love Song' is fuzzy in my memory, but the album didn't leave my car stereo for six months. Like a strung-out addict needing a fix, I needed to hear 'The Dancer' while driving recklessly down Chicago's highways in sync with the album's momentum. Simultaneously I scared my fellow passengers into loving it as much as I did. Nothing since U2's 'The Unforgettable Fire' put me in such a state, and nothing would again until The Frames' 'Fitzcarraldo' found its way to Vintage Vinyl in 1996.

Obsessed fan letter number 3 went something like this: In my bedroom listening to 'Revelate' at full volume, I whipped out some college-ruled notebook paper and poured my heart onto the blue lines. Using every pathetic cliché imaginable, I explained how songs like 'Revelate' and 'Fitzcarraldo' propelled my passion for music to yet another level. My letter even included a line comparing the band to picture frames and the art held within them. Had the letter survived to this day, it would have been good craic (Hey Glen, do you still have the note? It was bad enough to hold onto!). Sure that it would never reach its destination, I wasn't the least bit self-conscious about my animated ramblings.

Shortly after, the man himself called. Lead singer Glen Hansard calling me? Was my phone number in the letter? After recovering from the initial shock of receiving the call, our conversation reached dangerously high levels of music geekdom. We each weighed in on Chicago bands such as the Smashing Pumpkins and Glen recommended a long list of current favourite American bands that I should consider.

As an aspiring rock photographer, I already had amassed a portfolio of local bands. In later conversations with Glen, I expressed an eagerness to photograph The Frames. Rotting away at my day job in architecture, I heard about an upcoming Frames gig at The Olympia Theatre in Dublin. I convinced my friend Mike to book a flight there for a long weekend. Glen couldn't believe the news. 'Why the hell would you fly all the way from Chicago to Dublin to see us?'

In Ireland we first met with The Fat Lady Sings' Nick Kelly, who generously invited us to stay in his home. Seeing a familiar face before I was to meet Glen and the other lads eased my nerves a bit. We were on our way to a Frames rehearsal at The Factory when we stopped to buy the new issue of *Hotpress*. It had just come off the truck and I had the unique opportunity to watch Nick read the first review of his new solo record, 'Between Trapezes', which received a perfect 10/10 on the critical rating system. Ireland continued to work its magic in my life ... and I hadn't even met The Frames yet!

Finally, after celebrating over a couple of pints across the street, we made our way inside the maze of The Factory simply by following the sounds so familiar. I had no idea what it would be like to see the band perform live the songs that I raved about. Surprisingly it was very natural walking into the rehearsal space as the lads looked up, acknowledged us with a friendly nod and finished the track they were playing. I felt comfortable in the humble setting, as if I had seen them rehearse a hundred times before. This moment felt incredible; I was transported to a third dimension and my dream of seeing them in their home town became an instant reality. After that initial track they all walked over and introduced themselves graciously. This encounter felt more like a reunion rather than an introduction as we sat down for tea and caught up on life on both sides of the pond. I left rehearsal with images of Colm Mac Con Iomaire, Dave Odlum, Joe Doyle, Binzer and Glen plowing through the Pixies' 'Debaser', extremely satisfied that I found my way inside the frame rather than looking in from the outside.

The luck of the Irish struck again when later that evening Glen, Mike and I caught a one-way, don't-know-how-we'll-get-home ride to Kildare to catch another one of my must-see artists, Luka Bloom, performing an intimate pagan New Year gig for family and friends. Glen fetched his guitar for a couple of songs and then turned the attention toward me and my infamous fan letter, explaining how it felt to realise that his music reached people around the globe. The night ended ridiculously late (a kind of couldn't-get-enough late). To Luka's credit, he woke a local cab driver at 4am to drive us to Dublin.

Our next adventure led Mike and I to Whelan's for Nick's first solo gig there and then to The Olympia for our highly anticipated Frames experience. Our exhaustion evaporated as The Frames triumphantly took the stage. The hair-raising moments on record were more shattering live, surpassing every level of emotion that The Frames had ever taken me by. My heart raced from the sheer volume and force of Glen's guttural howls while simultaneously breaking with those melodramatic lyrics.

The first time I saw The Frames I had no idea who they were. They were playing what I now recognise as 'God Bless Mom' and it seemed that every person in the room knew the words but me.

It was a sold out show at Whelan's in February 1999. I was playing bass in a band that The Frames invited to Ireland to play two shows. As openers, our set went over predictably; many in front of the stage were genuinely glued to us but their attentiveness was drowned out by everyone else's indifference. The night ended in a room upstairs where a scant supply of beers was distributed to the lucky few (myself somehow included) and where there was no shortage of well wishers wondering what the hell the Americans were doing there.

My conversion to The Frames took some time. I had never gotten so close to music like theirs: sincere, bombastic, intimate, glorious, mighty rock. It didn't fit into my record collection too easily and it certainly didn't jive with the indie rock world I was immersing myself in at the time. By now I have been converted many times over and I identify with their sentiment more than with those who are too cool to sing along. God Bless Mom.

Dan Sullivan
Chicago

The Olympia Theatre / Dublin / 1997

Sweet home Chicago In 1999 Glen received his first opportunity to impress Chicago. Travel expenses kept the lads at home in Ireland while Glen debuted at Gunther Murphy's. After working tirelessly for months on booking venues for this monumental event, I missed the first gig because of some random stroke of misfortune. Luckily, Glen played at the Abbey Pub the following night and I returned to town in time for his performance. As I watched Glen serenade Chicago, I felt the start of what would become a second home for him and a pivotal point for The Frames' future in the United States.

Glen visited Chicago several times throughout the year, charming audiences and venue owners. Each visit influenced a larger, more appreciative audience. From the Hideout's indie essence to Schubas' intimate, cosy wood-panelled interior, Glen poured energy into these spaces that was rare among most performers. Somehow he continually increased his intense delivery. Whether he almost burst a blood vessel during a cover of Van Morrison's 'Astral Weeks' or thrashed his body around during a fuzzy guitar solo at the end of 'Stars Are Underground,' I have never seen one man with an acoustic guitar execute such a wide dynamic range.

After a chance visit to a record shop on the East Coast, Glen experienced his first taste of Songs: Ohia, a favourite band among serious Chicago music lovers. Smitten by lead singer Jason Molina's voice and the unique sound of his band, Glen asked him to tour with The Frames in Ireland and, as a result, the two musicians developed a strong friendship. Legendary recording engineer Steve Albini was partly responsible for producing this sound. Years earlier The Frames wanted Albini, best known for his work with Nirvana, P.J. Harvey and the Pixies, to produce 'Dance the Devil,' but, unfortunately because of politicking by their record label, The Frames were led to believe that scheduling conflicts spoiled the collaboration (yet another great move by the heads of corporate rock).

At Jason's urging, Glen called Albini and they finally connected for the first time in 1999. The highly successful 'For the Birds' recording sessions weren't yet a glimmer in The Frames' future but for one monumental day, Glen experimented in Albini's Electrical Audio studio.

Glen worked on new song ideas while living part time at Mike's apartment, fondly known as Hotel Jim (this is the same apartment often referenced during gigs in the introductory stories leading up to 'A Caution to the Birds'). He brought these half-formed ideas to Albini's studio where he led four musicians he had never previously played with, including Jason and Chicago musician Dan Sullivan, in an inspired session. All were vital contributors as Glen recorded new songs 'Disappointed' and 'A Caution to the Birds' in a sixteen-hour marathon session that lasted until 4am. Moreover, it was impossible to know then that the auburn-haired engineer named Rob Bochnik sitting behind the console would become the band's guitarist.

A witness to Glen's composing material on the fly, I turned to my camera to convey to others the vibe created in those moments. These recordings served as a turning point in The Frames' career as the songs that became 'For the Birds' morphed into the final product.

By the time the entire band surfaced in Chicago in autumn 1999, a fan base consisting of innocent concert goers recently spellbound by Glen and music-loving Chicago Irish grew exponentially. One gig in particular stands out in my mind – the Heritage Music Festival hosted by FitzGerald's, a historic venue on the city's West Side. Playing outside on a cool Halloween weekend underneath a tent, The Frames delivered a magical show, the kind of show that pulls in new faces – one of whom became my wife – and doesn't let them go until they've purchased the entire back catalogue and posted on the band's infamous online message board. Like countless others before her, Anita became an instant fan when she attended her first gig.

Timing is everything and a two-week window for all of The Frames to work with Albini in Chicago opened in autumn 2000. They recorded 'For the Birds' during this collaboration. I trolled the studio capturing as much as I could of the creative process. A dream came true as I lurked around corners, scoping for the perfect angle. Not only did I get to spend precious time with the band but also I was fortunate enough to hear new material. Ultimately I had myself positioned as a photographer exactly where and with whom I wanted, a huge personal accomplishment.

The sessions with Albini floated seamlessly. Despite the appearance that his attention is directed elsewhere, he is relaxed and in complete control. Once when the band gathered in the control room to play back a new edit, Albini, whose head had been buried in a science magazine, suddenly raised his eyes to make the most specific observation about what he just heard, never missing a note.

This proved to be a special time for The Frames. They were making a record without the help or interference of a major label and doing it on their own terms. 'For the Birds' became their most successful album to date, reaching number six on the Irish charts and culminating in a sweep of most of the honours in the *Hotpress* magazine readers' polls. But all that was unknown that fall as I tiptoed around wires and pedals to freeze those invaluable moments. Viewing those photos is a bit like slow motion. At the time I knew I had images that I'd be able to feel again long after they were developed in the lab.

The Abbey / Chicago / 1999

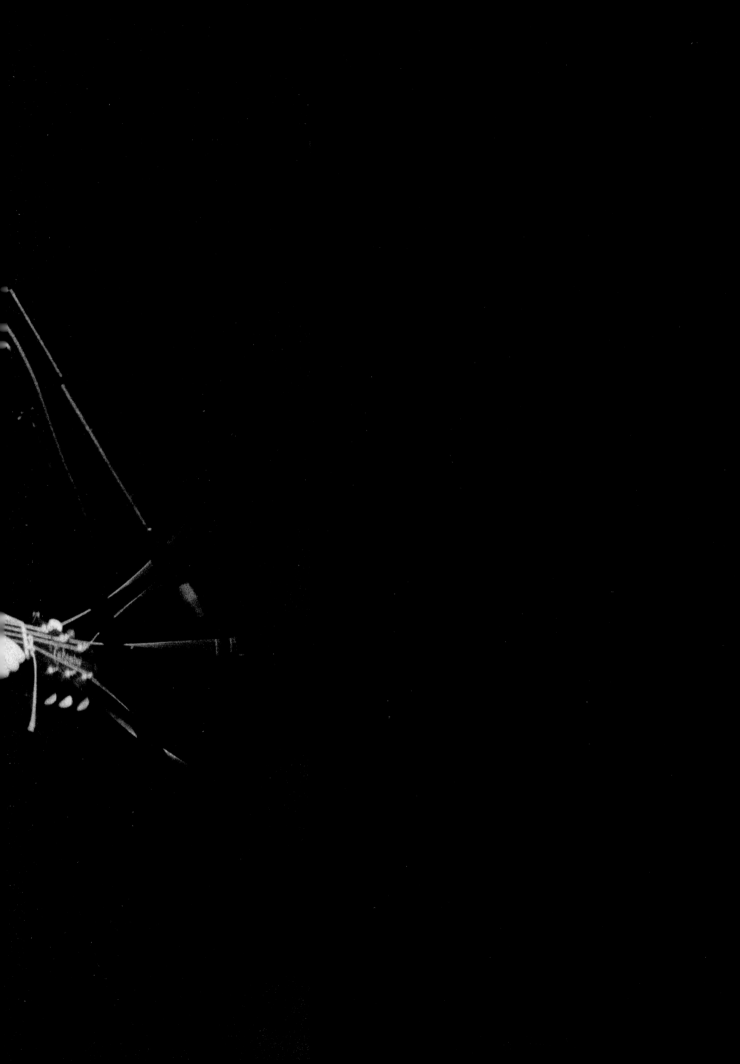

Elbo Room / Chicago / 1999

FitzGerald's / Berwyn, Illinois / 1999

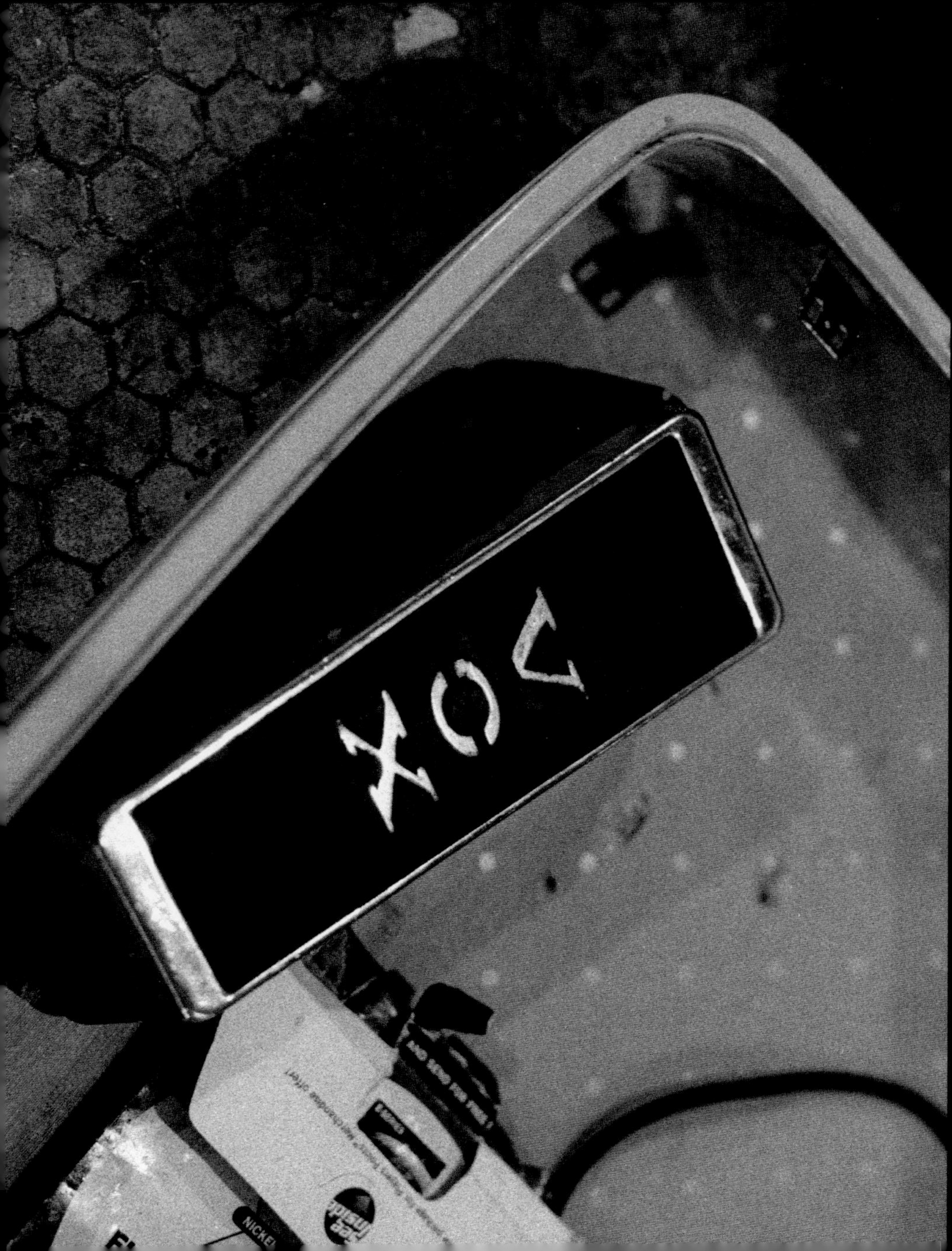

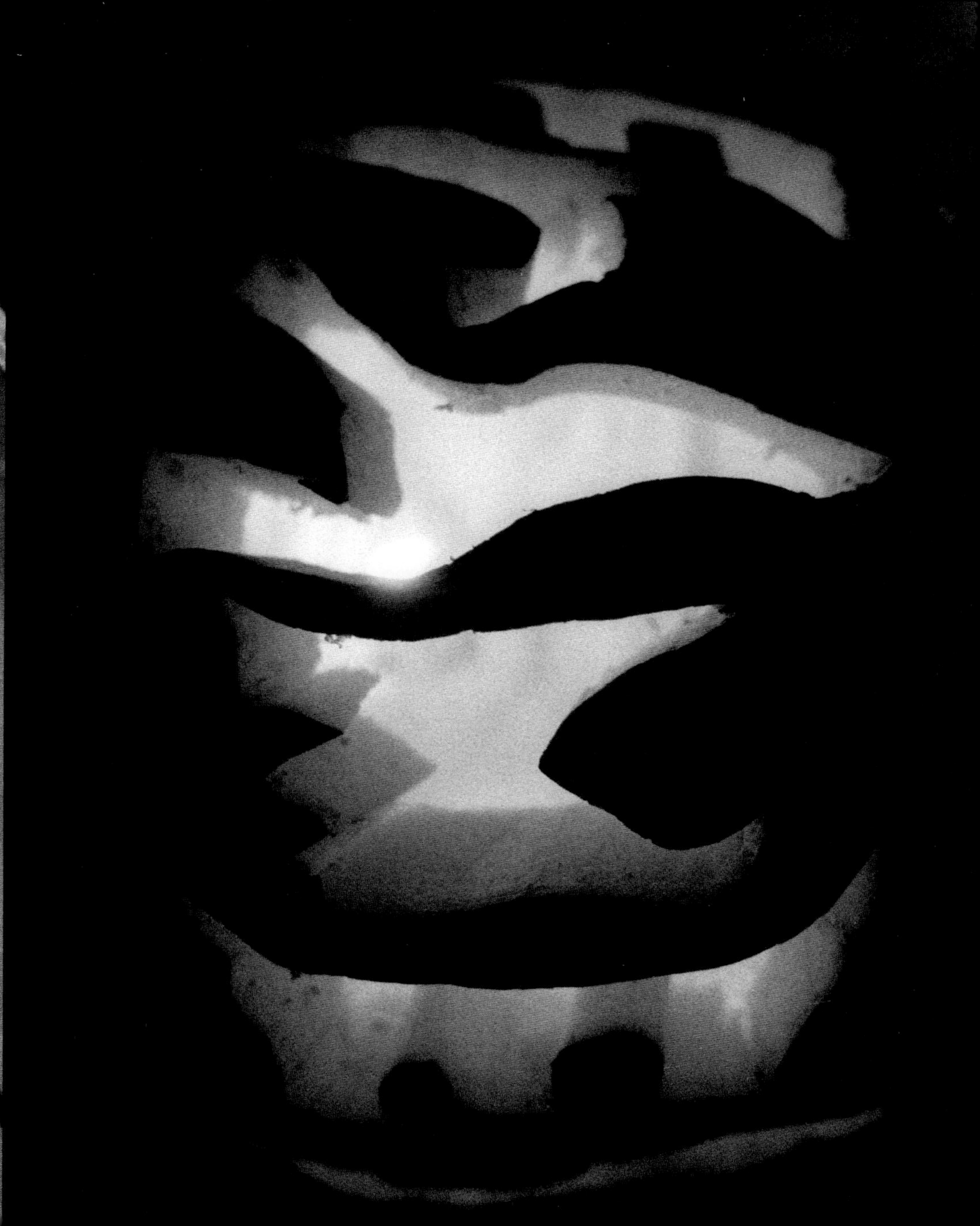

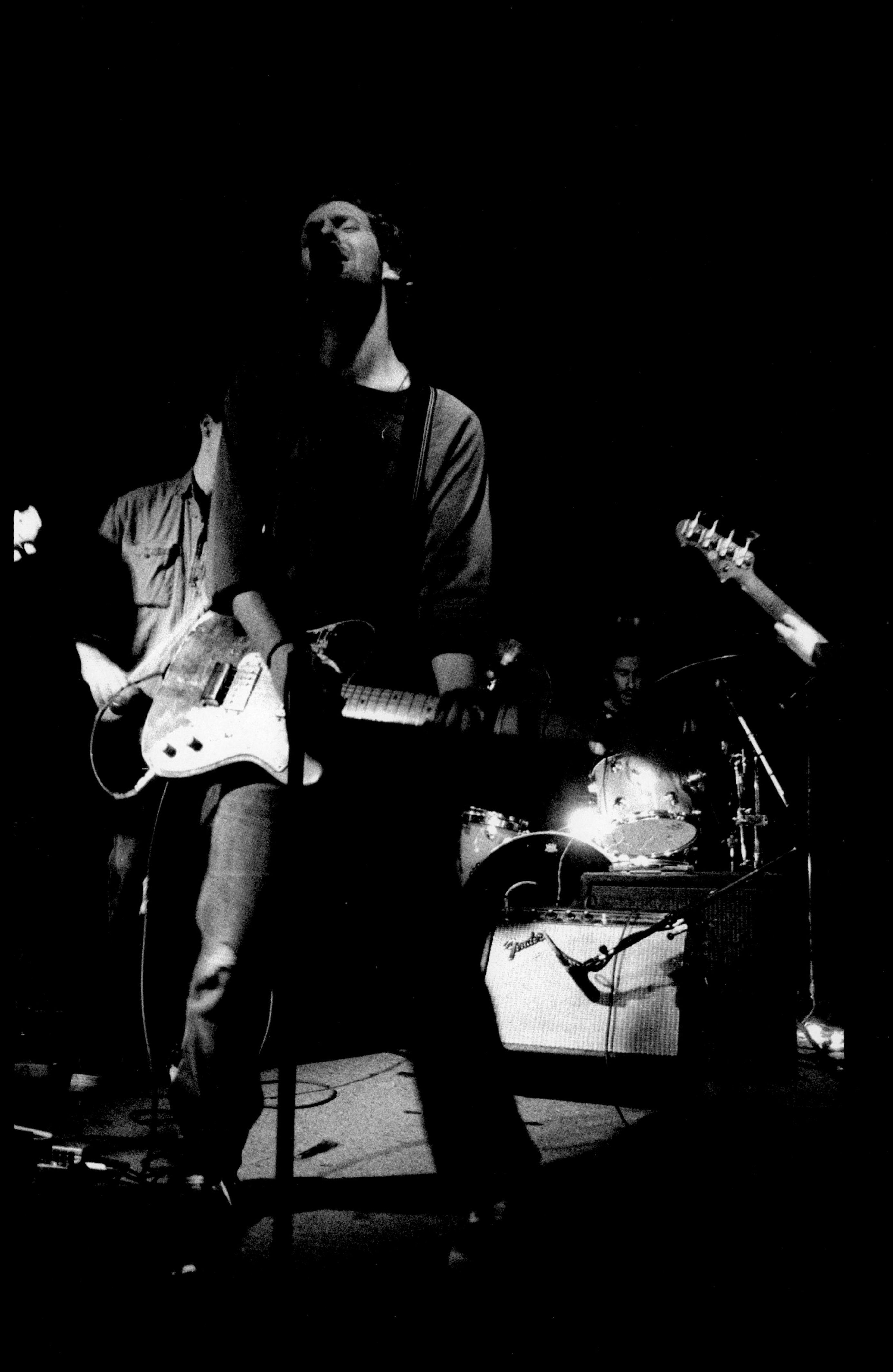

Gunther Murphy's / Chicago / 1999

Electrical Audio / Glen Hansard with Songs: Ohia / 2000

I met Glen Hansard on 23 May 2000. He had booked a day at Steve Albini's Electrical Audio to record in Studio B, where I worked as a staff engineer. Songs: Ohia, consisting of front-man Jason Molina, Jeff Panall (drums), Dan Sullivan (guitar) and Rob Sullivan (bass) backed him up.

I had known Dan and Rob Sullivan because I played in a group with them called The Butcher Shop Quartet. Jason and Dan had asked if I could engineer the session, so I signed up. In about twenty hours, we recorded and mixed six songs. I remember starting the session with the morning sun coming through the studio windows and ending the session with the morning sun once again peering through the windows. Glen really enjoyed his time there and immediately booked a session for The Frames to come and record later that year. I really enjoyed working on the session as well – it was great to be working with such good musicians. I never thought that Glen's and my path would meet again and change my life in such a profound way.

Rob Bochnik
The Frames, Dublin

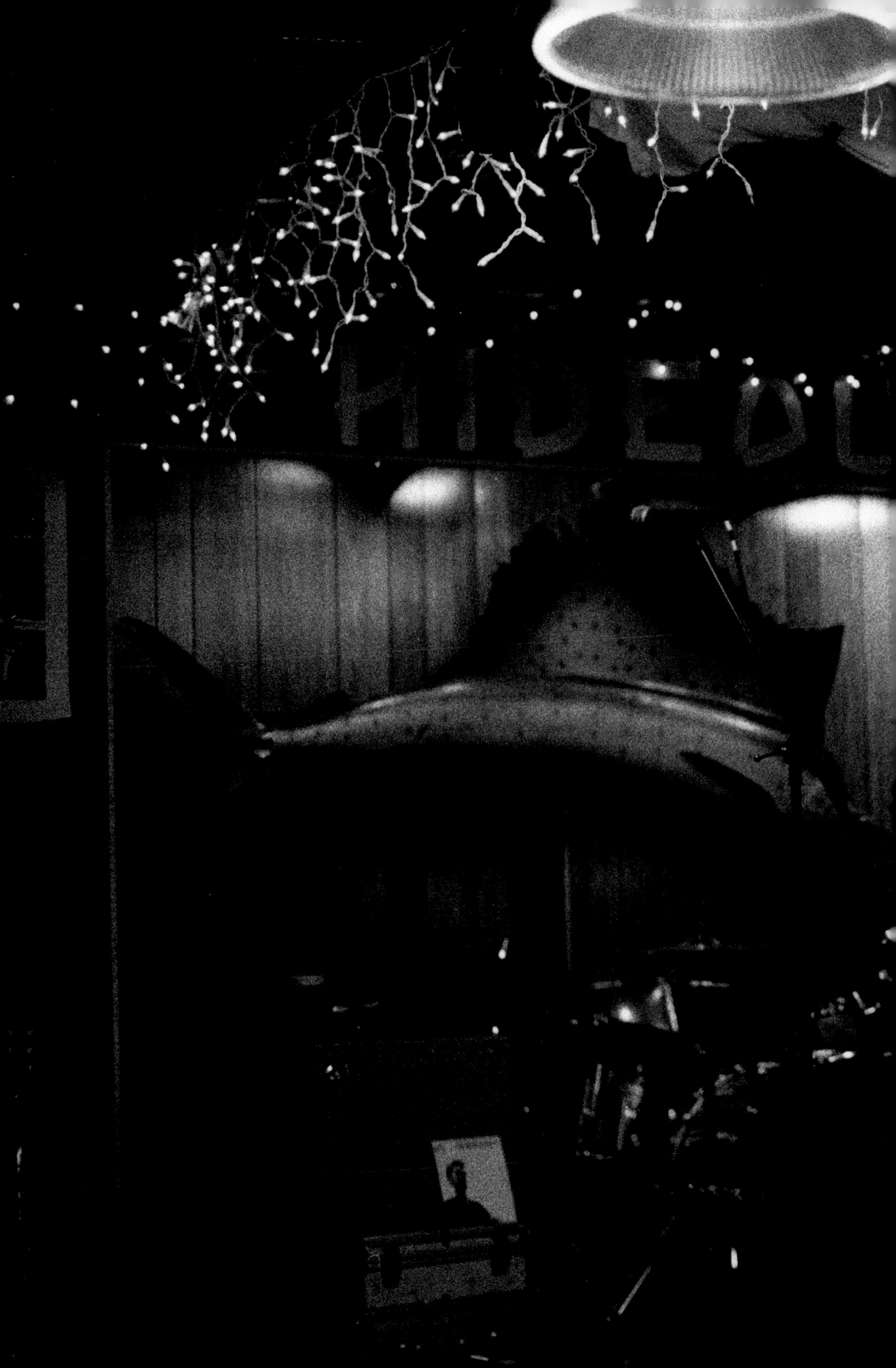

Hideout / Chicago / 2000

Electrical Audio / 'For The Birds' sessions / Chicago / 2000

With a wink and a smile and from a whisper to a thundering scream, Glen Hansard and The Frames have a way of emotionally involving you in every song. They are one of the most genuinely entertaining performers I've ever had the pleasure of hearing at Uncommon Ground. When Glen flew in to be a last-minute 'secret surprise' guest for the Jeff Buckley tribute concert, I literally had the hair stand up on the back of my neck multiple times during the evening. Please, please, please never miss Glen Hansard and The Frames whenever they come to your town.

Michael Cameron,
Uncommon Ground, Chicago

'Fitzcarraldo' was one of those albums that immediately grabbed you and wouldn't let you go. You simply couldn't get enough of this beautiful piece. If the album was vinyl, the needle would have grooved straight through; it was played constantly. So when Zoran suggested going to Dublin to see the band over a weekend, it made perfect sense.

This is just the kind of perfect sense Zoran often has. He casually had written Glen about how much he appreciated 'Fitzcarraldo' and offered his help building a Chicago fan base. Glen responded positively to the offer and it only seemed natural to head over to Dublin to meet the boys and share some pints. Any music lover will tell you it's the live experience that

seals the deal. The song, CD or collection of work any band releases crystallises in the live setting. So with a Guinness or two already under our belts, we walked into the mecca that was The Frames' rehearsal space and heard our first taste of the live deal. The visit came to a head at The Olympia Theatre show as the boys absolutely shredded the place. We experienced an insane weekend and our fellow fans quickly became our friends, and our fast friends in The Frames immediately became our brothers.

During the years my home has played host to Glen on his first visit to Chicago, as well as to the entire band and crew with what would have seemed at the time an overwhelming amount of sleeper sofas for one small apartment. Given that everyone eventually ended up with a bed or futon, some kind of a slapped-together sandwich, plenty of tea and a shower, the happy faces were never in short supply.

The music in the time that has gone by keeps getting better and the family bigger. The moments we share – be it a live show, long lunch or quick pint – are always cherished times. The friends and family we've gained will be with us always with the music we love at the core. Amen brother.

Mike Mondschein
occasional host, lifetime fan and friend, Chicago

Screenplay by Steve Albini

Cast:

Gerry – experienced road manager of good temper and strong voice

Glen (pronounced GLEnnh) – wide-eyed wanderer oozing lost-puppy charm

Colm (pronounced COLumm) – quiet, skin-covered skeleton who can divine the future, communicate with the dead and see the aura of mankind

Joe – pretty much what you'd expect from a Joe

Rob (pronounced Rzjobsceckujczi)– – beaming, cherubic, very happy to be here

Drummer – whoever's free at the moment

(Interior, hotel lobby. A clerk is talking on the telephone. A guest is reading a newspaper in an overstuffed chair.)

Clerk: No, they haven't arrived yet. I called the venue and they said they left some time ago. Well, if we have their deposit ... No, we haven't had anyone else asking about the rooms.

(Gerry walks in, wearing laminated tour passes around his neck and carrying a satchel.)

Clerk: I believe they're here now. Goodbye. (Hangs up telephone) May I help you?

Gerry: Do you have the rooms for the band? We may need another room tonight, I'll know in a minute.

Clerk: Just arrive from the venue then?

Gerry: Had a bit of a thing there. Do you know the band? (There is a commotion outside. Gerry calls over his shoulder) In here! (To Clerk, slightly irritated) Like herding cats up a rope ladder ... You'll have no trouble, I promise.

Clerk: May I have the names for the rooms?

Gerry: One for Rob Bochnik.

Clerk: Rob O'Chnik? Interesting name.

Gerry: Chicago, County Warsaw. One for Joe, one

for ... (Interrupted by Glen who enters wearing some really fucked-up secondhand clothes)

Glen: This the place? Right. Nice place. (Looks around) Not so used to nice places ...

Gerry: One for him. He's the singer. Do you know the band? Terrific presence. He can really hold an audience. Wait. (To Glen) Do we need the other room now?

Glen: Right. I lost her somewhere. People lose tings. Or trow 'em out. I lived off busking for a while, right. Can you believe the tings people trow out that are still good? I find the most amazing tings. Right, this shirt, can you believe someone trew it out? These shoes ...

Gerry: So no, is it? (Rumples nose) Stink o' benji off ya!

Glen: Right. I found my guitar. Someone just discarded it. The tings you can find if you look ...

Gerry (To Clerk): He found her, but then he lost her, so I guess we don't need the other room. Whatever that means.

Clerk: Terrific presence though, I agree.

Gerry: Do you know the band? Where was I?

Glen: ... I found a whole amplifier once ... (Picks up mobile phone from table next to guest reading newspaper. The phone obviously belongs to guest.) See what I mean? Right. Here's a perfectly good phone. (Opens phone and taps a key) Unlocked, and it's got minutes! (Glen starts dialing the phone and carries it around the corner)

Gerry: Is that five or six I've given you?

(Colm enters and looks around suspiciously.)

Gerry (To Colm): All right then?

Colm: Aye. (Still looking around) They're here. (Turns to Gerry) A double, so.

Gerry: Right then. (To Clerk) His'll be the double. Two beds. (Quietly to Clerk) One for the ghost, one for him. Apparently you've got a few here. Sometimes he brings his own. Either way, he takes a bed. And we'll need a bicycle pump.

Clerk (Confused): A bicycle pump?

Gerry: He's had a rough go in the bladders (Points to his lungs). Might need to top up. The valve's just there (Points to his nipple), flesh-coloured so. Can't see it without looking. Terrific work they do.

(Joe and Rob enter, chuckling at some unheard joke.)

Joe: Is the bar shut?

Clerk: I'm afraid so. There's a minibar in your room.

Joe: I have a room?

Clerk: I'm just getting the rooms now.

Gerry: Can you leave it for a minute, Joe?

Joe: It's all right, I've still got the rider in me bag. (Joe taps his bag and the clank of bottles can be heard inside) Good one tonight. The cheese wasn't so great. (Joe opens his bag, removes a bread roll and a wedge of cheese and begins making a crude sandwich with them) I almost didn't bother.

Rob: Can I have one of those?

Joe: I wouldn't bother. (Takes a bite of his sandwich) Honestly, not worth your time.

Gerry (Discreetly to the group): Are we havin' porno tonight?

Rob: Pierogies?

Gerry (Louder, emphatically): Are we havin' porno tonight?

All: Aye.

Gerry (To Clerk): Can you unlock the in-room movies then? Just a moment. (Turns to Colm) And yours?

Colm: They'd rather not.

Gerry (To Clerk): Except his. (Corrects himself) Theirs. Ghosts don't go for porno. Frustrates them.

Clerk (Confused): So that's four singles, one double, singles with in-room movies, double without, a bicycle pump ...

Gerry: Five singles.

Clerk: Five?

Gerry: Let me check. (To the group) Do we have a drummer?

(The group, perplexed, confers for a moment. Just then, Drummer walks in looking startled, having overheard his existence being questioned. The group sees him then answers decisively) Yes, yes.

Gerry: Right then. We have a drummer so, that's another room then. Glad I checked.

Glen (Re-enters, talking on his new mobile phone): ... Right. Right. (Long pause) Right. Right then. (Closes phone) Gerry, can I get that room?

Rob: Wow, that's a nice phone.

Glen: Found it. Minutes and all.

Gerry (To Clerk): One of the singles is now a double. Wait. (To Glen) Porno?

Glen: Right, let me tink ... No, I tink.

Gerry (To Clerk): Without ...

Glen (Interrupting Gerry): Better safe than sorry. I don't know what she's into ...

Gerry: Right. (To Clerk) Leave it on.

Glen: Could come in handy ...

Gerry (To Glen): So you found her again?

Glen: No, I just hit a few numbers in speed dial. One of them. Anita, I tink. Maybe Allison. I didn't have to go past the As, I know that. Find out when she gets here. Amazing what you find ...

Steve Albini
Electrical Audio, Chicago

EXIT

Uncommon Ground / Chicago / 2000

Glen and the band could have been better friends to us all.

They could have helped more, cared more, given more, worked more, dropped into our lives all a little sooner. Somehow, it ends up that they were out all along doing something as useless as following the song. You don't eulogise your friends that are still kicking. Alas, I've been asked to do basically this and – like Glen has taught me in all of those hundreds of songs and hours spent in company – anyone who follows songs is putting all of that love right back into the work, back into the world. So I've been trying to do that all these years.

It is 3 o'clock or so in the morning, boys. I'm under a nearly full moon here in Chicago and wanted to get to writing a new song. It's fall and I know Glen might come up with lines about how, 'All the shadows are still with us. All the smallest sad things fall like giants'. I was trying to think of something to say that looked good in words but I'm out here looking for a song, too. I know wherever The Frames are that they are doing the same. I think now of my friends to be, who heard my first record in a shop in Philadelphia. I think of how I wish I'd been there to give the thing to them instead of their buying it. All that happened in the end was that Glen found an obscure songwriter and he and the band brought me to Ireland, put a guitar in my hand, put my ass in the car and said, 'Let's go'!

I hope that, however this book ends up, it can put some of you into that older, deeper, darker world that is in all of these songs.

Harmony onward, friends.

Jason Molina

Songs: Ohia

Magnolia Electric Co., Chicago

Metro / Chicago / 2000

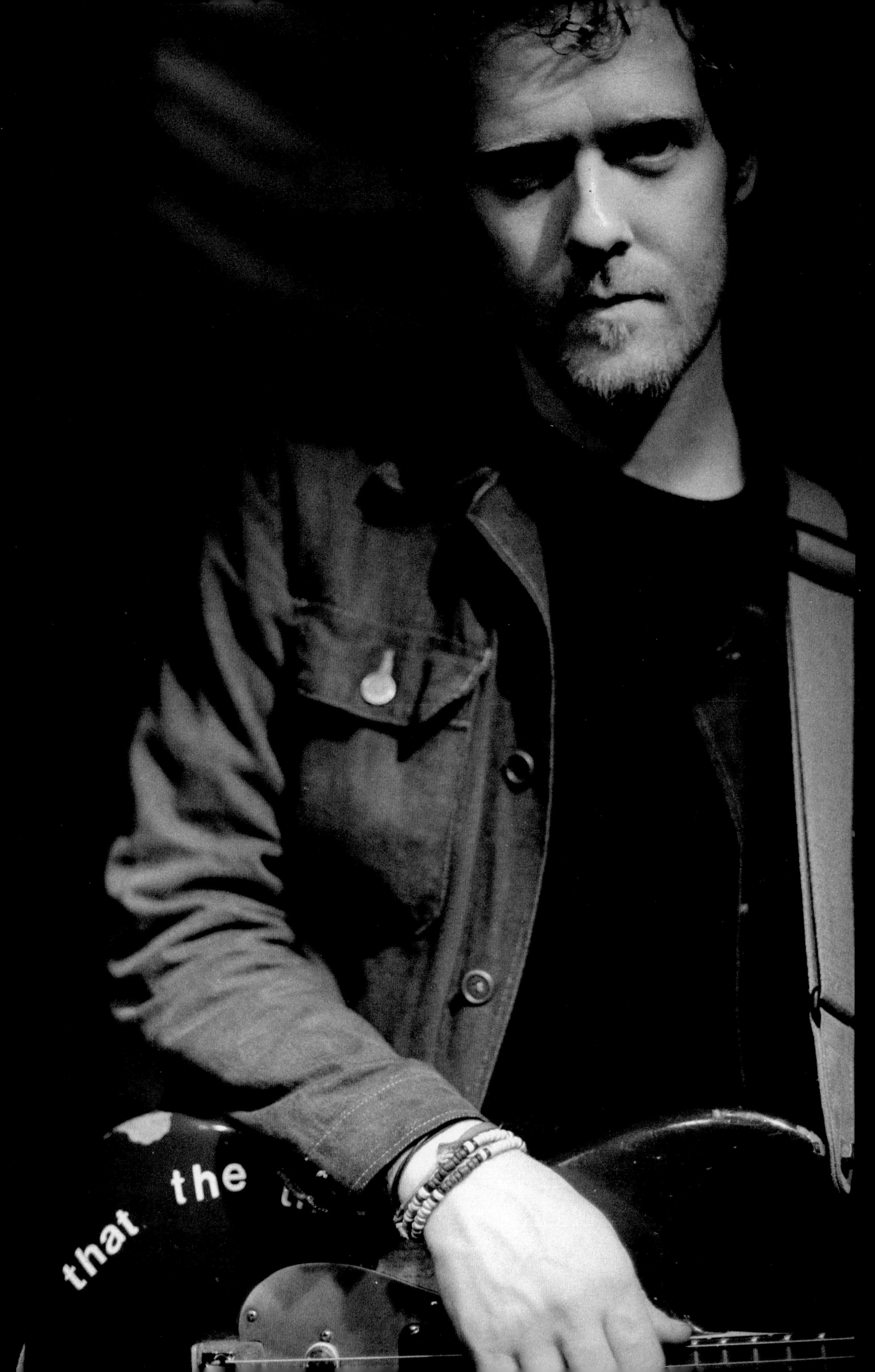

Hideout / On Stage Photo Session / Chicago / 2001

I first met Glen with my good friend and Chicago disc jockey Richard Milne, who already was aware of The Frames thanks to Zoran Orlić's zealous persistence. Glen played a solo gig at Uncommon Ground in Chicago, which is right around the corner from my club, Metro.

Following an impressive set, Glen walked up to Richard and the introductions began. I loved what I had heard that night and after learning that he had a band back home, I was convinced we'd be working together in the near future – solo or not.

Within a year of meeting him, I headed to Dublin to see my friends Smashing Pumpkins complete their final tour as a band at The Olympia Theatre. After having spent a day at U2's headquarters, it was time to take in Dublin properly. Susan Hunter of Principle Management hosted me with a fabulous dinner and plenty of drinks and then took me to Whelan's to see one of her management artists, Mundy. I fell in love with Mundy's sound and the vibe was mind-blowing at this Dublin mecca of Irish music.

Out of nowhere, Glen appeared at Whelan's and said, 'Hey Joe, we met in Chicago ...' I was blown away that he remembered me and we just picked up where we left off. At this point there was no reason to leave the confines of this amazing musicians' sanctuary where it literally seemed that all of Ireland's greatest bands had congregated under one roof that night.

I remember sitting upstairs in the Green Room with a fire crackling while the artists multiplied and passed around a guitar in between endless pints of Ireland's finest spirits. This forever will define the Irish experience for me as I had been baptised into the local Irish rock 'n' roll music scene.

Joe Shanahan
Metro, Chicago

A few years ago Glen Hansard and some of The Frames dropped by the Hideout for some pints. I think they were making a record with Steve Albini. Glen picked up someone else's guitar and played some impromptu songs. Over time The Frames would drop in after shows or play at the Hideout. It was always fun and informal.

A couple of years ago, my wife Katie and I were going to Ireland for the Galway Arts Festival. We asked Glen about places to go in Dublin. He told us about different pubs and mentioned that The Frames were playing a festival while we would be there. He said we should come by, he'd put our names on the guest list. Months went by and we hadn't seen Glen or anything. We went to Ireland, but I didn't do any homework like I usually do before a trip. We got to Dublin on a Friday, and Saturday morning we caught a packed bus for the Witness Festival. There were thousands of people and the lines were a mile long. We were prepared to pay, but we saw a trailer that said VIP. We walked up and asked if we were on The Frames' list. We were handed two all-access passes – backstage, everything. Glen had remembered after a drunken conversation at the Hideout two months earlier.

There must have been 100,000 people and ten stages. The Frames were headlining a stage. They packed the area when they played. I would guess at least 5,000 people, all singing every word of their songs. When we went backstage, they were sitting with all these big bands from the UK and Ireland. They hugged us, offered us pints and treated us like visiting royalty. They told the people they were with about how great Chicago is, the cool bars and the great music scene. They were totally nice. I just had no idea how huge they were in Ireland; I had only seen them at Chicago bars and they never let on. It was a great day. A big picture of The Frames appeared on the cover of the Dublin Sunday newspaper the next day.

I saw the guys last year at our friend's house. They were all sitting in the kitchen, eating sandwiches, drinking pints and talking about movies and the government – just like at the Witness Festival. Whether it was in front of 5,000 folks, a bunch of hip UK bands backstage or in a kitchen in Chicago, The Frames are regular guys. That is why The Frames are honorary Chicagoans. They have made us their sister city. They hang out here like locals and they promote us when they are at home in Dublin. They are truly a band of the people, by the people and for the people.

Tim Tuten
Hideout, Chicago

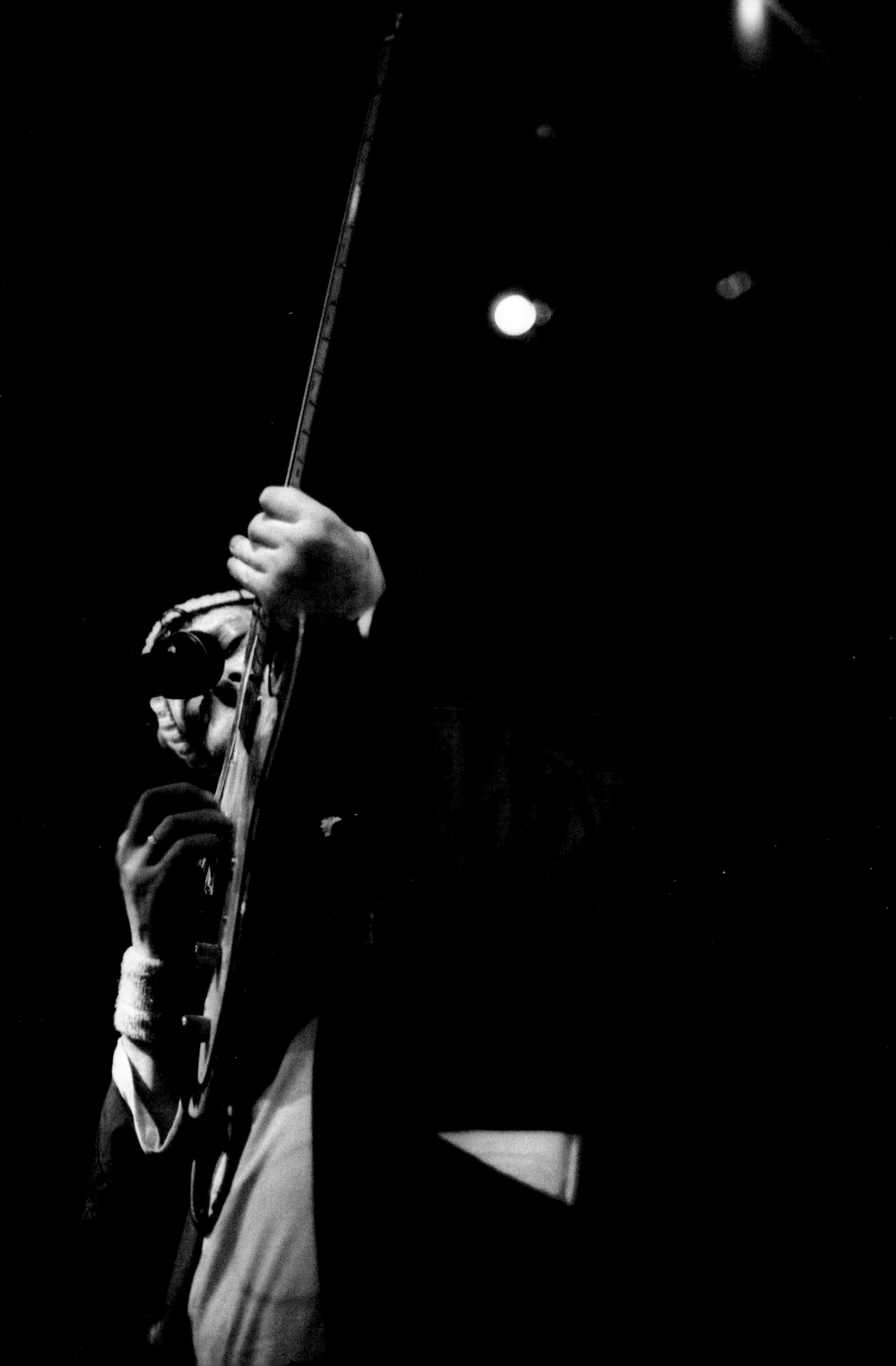

The High Dive / Champaign, Illinois / 2002

Touring the States

In 2002 Frames manager Claire Leadbitter asked me to manage the band's first US headlining tour. Never having been a tour manager, I was extremely nervous even though the band and I had become good friends.

Driving 10,000-plus miles on a 32-day tour in a mini van and a recreational vehicle would wear on anyone's nerves. Co-ordinating travelling logistics became the biggest challenge. No matter how invigorating the live shows were night after night, I constantly worried about arriving on time for the next city's sound check. Check-in at hotels routinely occurred around 3am and getting the lads out of bed only a few hours later to continue the trip was virtually impossible. At least two members of the group inevitably would be raring to go but the majority resisted my persistent wake-up calls. Since food usually got everyone moving, I used it as a constant motivator, although it can be difficult to get excited about the roadside diners scattered across America.

Personal CDs were a hot commodity throughout the tour to be traded, stolen, recommended and listened to repeatedly among all of us. The sounds of Beck, Wilco, The Wedding Present and Robbie Robertson drowned out the monotony of the road for hours. I constantly would lose bass player Joe and Glen to record stores where they would fetch new collections of music to expand our tour library.

Revelations awaited us around every corner, but none more so than when we arrived in Atlanta to find fellow Irishmen and long-time mates Ash. The band was in town opening for Coldplay at a large outdoor arena. Nasty weather forced them to cancel the show, and we hoped Ash might drop by The Frames' gig so both homesick bands could catch up. To our surprise, towards the end of The Frames' set, Ash appeared onstage after quietly enjoying the gig from the back.

Though thrilled with the spontaneous performance, my paranoia as tour manager took over and thoughts that the gig could go on forever raced through my head. We had a sound check the next day in New Orleans, a ten-hour drive away, and – assuming the lads make it to bed by 5am – how will the entourage get there on time? On the other hand, Ash is onstage with The Frames for a full-blown jam session and Coldplay's Chris Martin is standing behind me anxiously waiting his turn. No longer able to ignore my camera, I loaded roll after roll of film so as not to miss The Frames, Ash and Chris winging it on an array of classic rock songs. The photos speak volumes about why a stressful, speed limit-busting trip to New Orleans was completely worth every painful minute of driving.

My fantasy has been to capture a band on tour in still frame for everyone out there who lives vicariously through stories and images of life on the road. Between driving, eating, shopping and playing a gig almost nightly, photo shoots were rare but somehow I gathered the group in scenes throughout the tour's landscape. Specific places stand out in my memory where time, light and environment fell perfectly into place.

For example, at a venue in Denton, Texas, Glen and I broke away before a routine sound check and headed for an old abandoned train depot. We have a rule: no fake expressions or forced poses, or I'd slip the camera into my shoulder bag. The goal always is to be natural. If I suspect he is giving me a helping of cheesiness, I stop and we laugh because he knows he's not being true to the moment. Glen and I were both in sync as we spontaneously vanished into the old ghost town. Infinite deserted space within a prairie background decorated the landscape behind us. A decaying rope hanging from the old depot roof served as the perfect prop for Glen getting 'hung' by his neck in true Texas style. We walked through slowly only to stumble upon chunks of jagged tree and a random piece of leather shaped like old '80s Porsche sunglasses, which fit Glen's face perfectly. Sessions like this can never be planned or rehearsed.

Driving through the southern California desert on our way to San Diego, we stopped at mammoth sand dunes looming in the 110-degree heat. Foreheads dripping with sweat, feet burning in Converse sneakers, Glen and the lads trudged through the slippery sand slopes until they finally reached one of the peaks where I shot them before someone nearly passed out from dehydration. The view of the overlapping sand seemed endless as we all secretly enjoyed the silence and stillness of the desert. I positioned the lads into one pose but the rest of the images came from them sitting down taking a break. Then I snapped more shots of them trotting back to the vehicle for some much-needed cold air blowing through the vents.

One of my favourite photo sessions occurred in the Badlands of South Dakota. I captured ironic footage of a band full of life and love against a harsh, barren landscape that forever will be imprinted in my memory. We all felt the spirit of the region while visiting the Crazy Horse Memorial and Little Bighorn Battlefield National Monument, paying unspoken homage to the Native American tradition heavy in this land.

Driving through the Great Plains, Chicago slowly came into sight. The marathon tour was about to end with the last and biggest gig at the legendary Metro with Cinerama. Practically stripped of all my duties, I sat back with a beer and reflected on the amazing experience. The next morning, before the lads' flight to Ireland, we planned a proper studio photo shoot for an Irish magazine cover. Unlike the spontaneous, candid photos taken during the tour, in this session we were all able to catch our breath collectively and relax, a testament to the hectic last 30 days. In retrospect, no one would have guessed I shot a bunch of tired faces that day. Must have been the rock 'n' roll glow. With the tour completed and the lads on their way home, I thought I could rest without worrying about a schedule, but my mind continued to play dirty tricks. Every night for the next two weeks I bolted out of bed convinced the band was in the adjacent room late for the next gig. Looking back, I acquired a newfound respect for what bands go through coming off a tour and trying to assimilate to everyday life (it's not that glamorous).

USA Tour / 2002

USA Tour / The Badlands, South Dakota / 2002

USA Tour / Denton, Texas / 2002

A tribute to Mic Christopher Musicians and music fans alike in Ireland will never forget the tragic death in 2001 of The Frames' long-time friend Mic Christopher. The charismatic singer fronted the Mary Janes before striking out on his own to release a four-song EP containing the uplifting 'Hey Day'. While on tour with the Waterboys to promote his newfound solo career, Mic took a tumble down a flight of stairs, which left him in a coma. Attending the launch of Mic's posthumous album 'Skylarkin' at Vicar Street on 29 November 2002 remains one of the most spiritual moments of my life.

I arrived in Dublin a couple days earlier for a series of Frames gigs that later comprised the track listing of 'Set List'. A buzz pulsed throughout the city as I stepped off the plane, culminating in the boundless outpouring of love by Mic's family, friends and fans at a Frames' tribute concert for their dear friend. This was no place for grieving, so much of which had permeated the previous year. This was a celebration of a life lived and missed and of the songs that will ensure an immortal place in the history of Irish music.

The faces of his parents, Harry and Vaun, and his sister Maureen as they entered the stage to deafening applause from a fan-filled crowd were a testament to the innocent energy of Mic's colourful life. My camera recorded moment after moment, one more exhilarating than the next: Damien Rice and Lisa Hannigan kneeling in reverence, Colm Mac Con Iomaire reeling with Kila before joining The Frames and Mic's former bandmates from the Mary Janes.

I chatted with Mic once, mostly about his volunteer mission to Bosnia with War Child. That brief conversation took on a profoundly different meaning when the video for the title track played to the darkened room. Mesmerised by clips of footage that Mic had taken, I put my camera down, unable to move, feet frozen. In slow motion children played in a school yard, naturally expressing their pure, blind love and joy in the most routine act, an innocence that Mic cherished. This simplicity was magic to Mic and everyone in that room felt his powerful spirit. I'll never hear 'Skylarkin' again without those moving images flickering through my mind as a reminder of Mic's humble and nurturing soul.

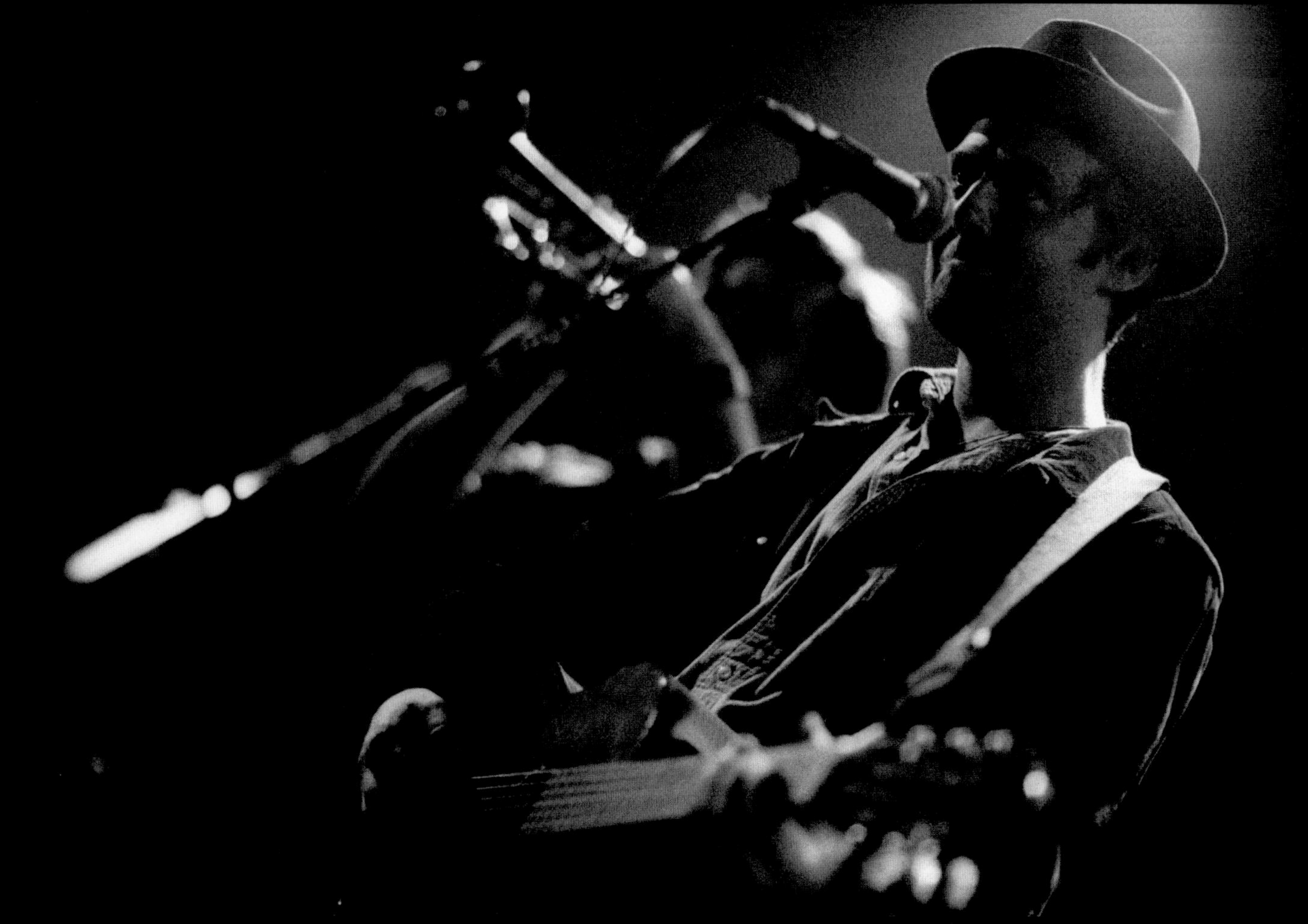

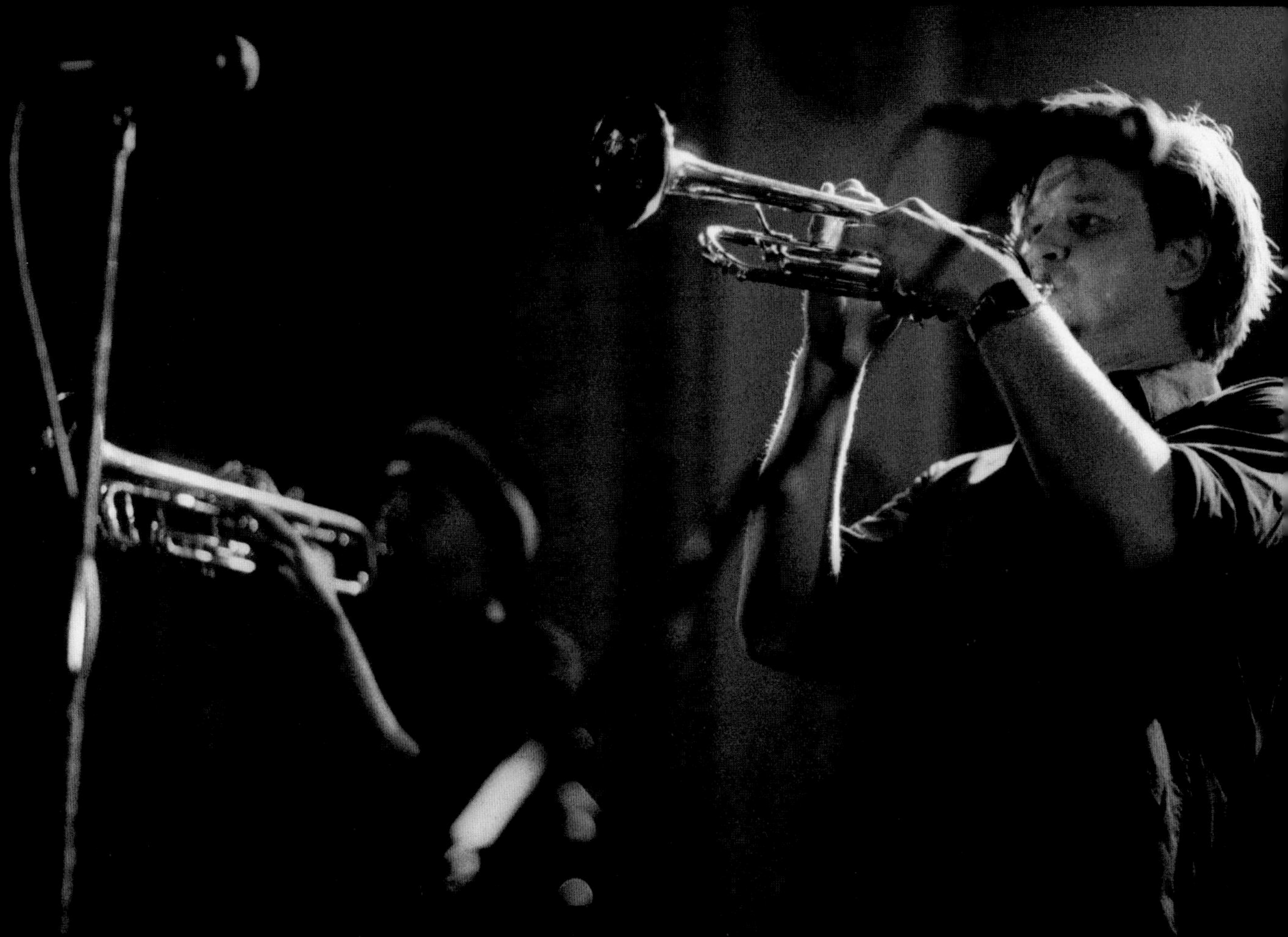

Metro / The Frames with Calexico / Chicago / 2003

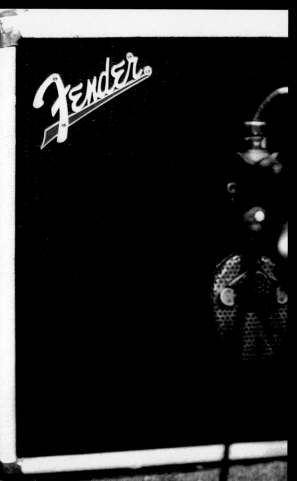

Ship caught in the bay :

finally : Vocal, ~~the~~ ~~the~~ the

a caution 1:13 : reverse noodles,

happy : Vocal, harmonie

the blood :

fake : ~~No vox~~ No vox

keepsake : Piano, Vocal, Violins

Concentric : acc. vocal, harmon

Locusts : vocal fixes, strin

dream awake : Vocal, banjo

Instrumental ♫

:

Suffer in Silence

: Vocal,

People get ready

: Vocal, riff,

Sad Songs

: Record..

Simple Question

are You Sleeping? : Vocal, String

Brooklyn Bridge Shoot / New York City / 2004

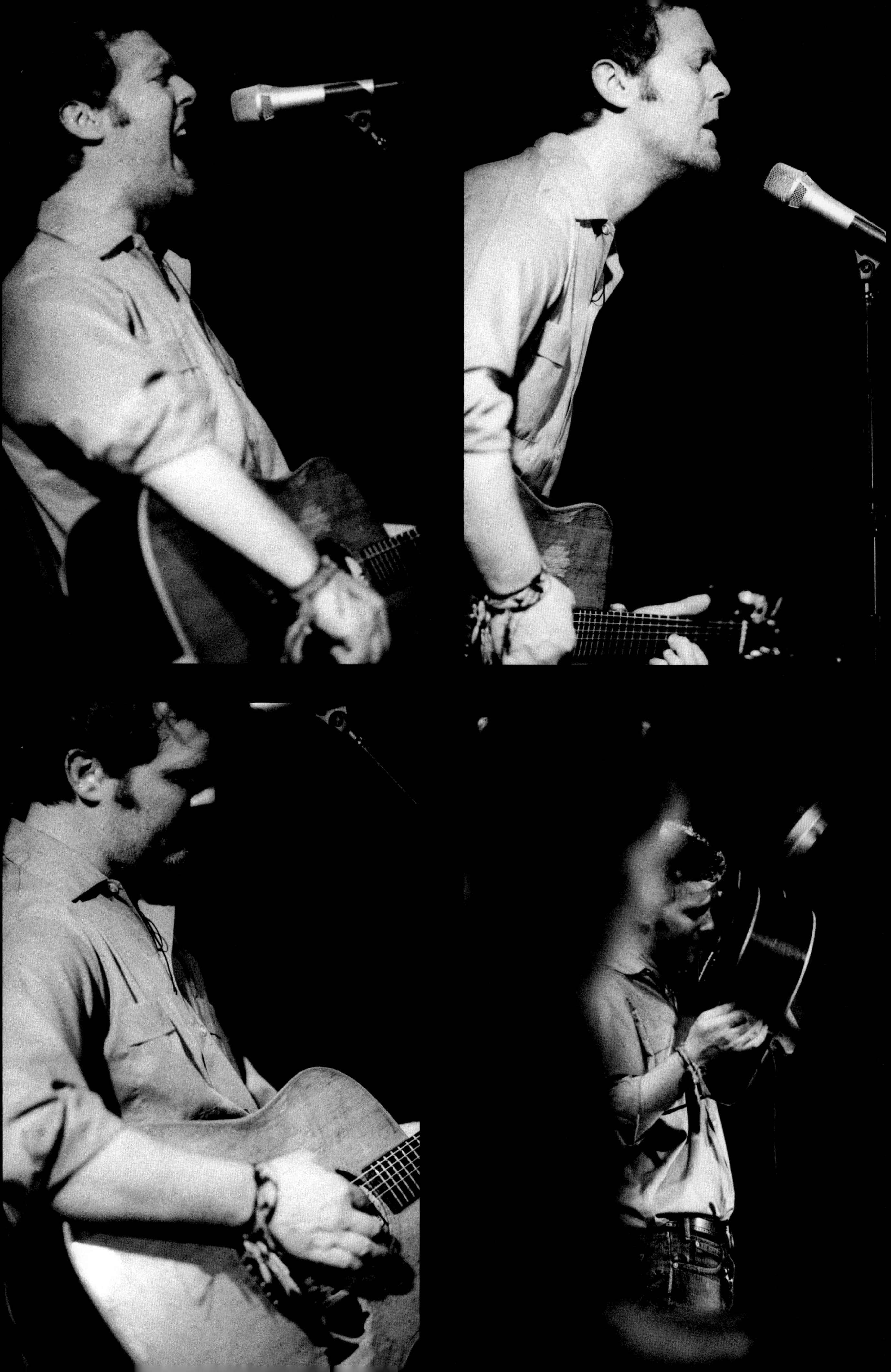

Martyrs / Glen Hansard and Marketa Irglova / Chicago / 2005

'Austin City Limits' Festival / Austin, Texas / 2005

The lads didn't disappoint. Glen's emotional voice sailed through the vast, dimly-lit hall like a lone ship in the darkness of the ocean. A natural storyteller who is alternately quiet and funny, he referenced both a raving lunatic and the Bible in his discourse with the audience.

Admittedly selfish, I mourned the days when it felt like I had The Frames all to myself. Things are different now. Manoeuvrings around the stage trying to capture multiple angles of Glen and the lads in rock star poses is close to impossible. Gone are the days when a few loners would stalk the front row with apprehension while the rest hung back in the spotlight's shadows. Today, fans clamour for the best spot and my camera and I are forced to compete with them. These emotions are hard to explain without sounding unsupportive of their success. Maybe this sense of loss is similar to what a parent feels when watching a child grow up and leave home to explore the world. It's a bittersweet combination of pride and anxiety.

Today, it all makes sense to me. I became aware of a powerful musical force and attempted to share this discovery with others by lining up gigs and documenting the artistic process unfolding. It's a sweet feeling when I can capture a fleeting moment of passion through the lens while watching new faces surrender to something unexpected colliding with their innermost emotions.

As a chapter ends for The Frames and myself, a new one also begins. Throughout the years, friendships have been forged, romances kindled, wisdom gained, foolishness and folly expelled, all through the spectrum of my uncommon relationship with The Frames. Their music has provided the soundtrack for a good portion of my life as it has for many fans. I'm honoured and privileged to have been a small part of their evolving career. As more fans emerge and larger venues vie for the band, I'm anxious and waiting to view *The Frames behind the glass.*

Reflections from behind the glass
This book almost ended in December 2004 when I met the lads in New York City for what was to be a final photo shoot. I realised after seeing those images that this book needed to end in Chicago, The Frames' second home. So I returned to Chicago and waited until they came to me.

In March 2005 Glen played a few solo dates before joining the rest of the band for a short festival stint across the United States. For the first time in what seemed like ages, Glen performed to a small, rapt audience at Martyrs. Every note rang out in a flurry of passion, piercing the eerie silence of the pub where even the typical clanking of bottles at the bar had succumbed to the music. Struck by a strange sense of déjà vu, I reminisced about the years past and felt a twinge of nostalgia as Glen hauntingly serenaded us with 'Rise', which was recorded in 2000 on a dark Thanksgiving night with Albini.

The entire band returned again in November 2005 to play at Park West with Josh Ritter opening, creating a new memory in the rich history of their performances. Former Frames' drummer Dave Hingerty, my US tour co-pilot, now stood on stage with Josh's band, and all of a sudden these worlds came full circle in a sentimental experience.

I staked my position near the front of the stage to collect some images. Behind me, an uninitiated fan politely inquired if I was going to stand there the whole night. Trembling from the idea of seeing live this band that he stumbled upon in his favourite online magazine, he anxiously waited for The Frames to fulful his high expectations. I chuckled to myself remembering those innocent days, having graduated from the same school of heady fanaticism. But I held off and maintained my veteran credentials while I gently warned him that he was about to get his fucking mind blown away.